CONQUERING THE MOUNTAIN THAT IS YOU

The Downfall of Damaging Habit and Overcoming Self-sabotaging

By

GW00671735

Judson Pugh

Techniques for Improving Self-awareness and Self-Regulation

How to overcome setbacks and cultivate resilience

INTRODUCTION

When Pugh obtained a position at a prestigious financial services company, his career appeared to be moving in the right direction. But after a few early successes, he started making terrible choices and jeopardizing his own career. A cycle of self-sabotage and underachievement eventually developed as a result of negative thought patterns and fear of the unknown.

People like Pugh display the typical characteristics of the "golden larva"; they have the potential for a prosperous future but ultimately limit their capacity to grow. A self-sabotaging person is like a caterpillar that never reaches its full potential and never becomes a butterfly.

An unreasonable fear of failing is one of the key reasons individuals like Pugh find themselves in a rut in life. Such people generally shy away from taking chances or trying anything if there is a chance of failing. This dread, which frequently stems from failures in the past or embarrassing or demeaning situations, can exacerbate a number of emotional and psychological issues, such as anxiety, panic attacks, and depression.

Although it is a unique phenomenon, fear of success is frequently mistaken for fear of failure. People who are afraid of succeeding put barriers in their way to slow down their progress. Success itself doesn't paralyze; rather, it's the implications that follow. People are concerned about the social effects of being overly conspicuous or fear they won't be able to handle the attention. They occasionally have self-limiting ideas, such as the notion that they are not deserving of achievement, or they can worry about standing out from others who are equally or more deserving.

These types of phobias can be established from childhood and persist into maturity. People worry about falling short of unreasonable expectations because they fear being held to them, or they worry that their accomplishments will be overlooked because they are successful. Because of this, individuals defend themselves by giving up or acting in ways that hinder their progress.

Imposter syndrome, in which people mistrust their skills and feel undeserving of their accomplishments, can coexist with a dread of both failure and success. Imposter syndrome patients frequently downplay their accomplishments and blame luck or other outside reasons for their success. Perfectionism can exacerbate feelings of inadequacy and imposter syndrome. Anxiety, despair, and even burnout can emerge from a continual need for approval from others. This behavior may have its roots in a childhood when success was equated with self-worth and undue emphasis was placed on achieving.

The Peter Pan syndrome, or the unwillingness to mature and assume adult responsibilities, is another underlying cause of self-sabotage. People who want to live in "Neverland" avoid the difficulties that come with becoming an adult, are unmotivated, are afraid of commitment, and are uninterested in their profession. They deflect responsibility for mistakes by offering justifications or pointing the finger at others.

These people are therefore prone to endanger their own careers. This might be the result of their upbringing, in which their parents protected them from the "dangers" of the outer world or careers who let them act however they pleased without repercussions. The mindset and abilities required for a smooth transition into adulthood may never be developed in children raised by either overly lenient or overly protective parents.

CHAPTER ONE

Understanding Self-Sabotage

Self-sabotage is a puzzling and frequently sneaky psychological action that might obstruct our success and growth in life. It involves behaviors, attitudes, or ways of thinking that, frequently without our awareness, work against our own objectives and wellbeing. A critical first step toward personal development and self-improvement is understanding self-sabotage.

Self-sabotage primarily results from our internal anxieties and beliefs. It feels like there is an invisible force pulling us away from the very things we want. This conduct generally results from low self-esteem, unresolved childhood trauma, or ingrained limiting views about our value and potential. Procrastination is among the self-sabotage behaviors that are most frequently seen. We could have a chore or a goal we want to complete, but we frequently put it off or come up with reasons not to start. This procrastination frequently hides a fear of either achievement or failure. We cannot succeed but also cannot fail if we never start.

Negative self-talk is another kind of self-sabotage. This refers to the mental discourse in which we constantly berate ourselves for past errors, mistrust our own ability, and condemn our own judgment. When we believe we can't succeed, we are less inclined to put up the effort necessary to accomplish our goals, which leads to a self-fulfilling prophesy.

Relationships can be affected by self-sabotage. Some people may reject potential acquaintances or relationships out of fear of being wounded or rejected. They could start arguments or emotionally retreat, which makes their concerns become self-fulfilling prophecies.

Introspection is necessary to understand self-sabotage. Investigating your own ideas, attitudes, and actions is crucial. Consider asking yourself, "What am I afraid of? Why do I question my skills? When did I begin to think I wasn't good enough? The first step in overcoming self-sabotage is to pinpoint its underlying causes.

Theories of Self Sabotage

Psychoanalysis, sociology, psychology, and psychiatry all have a role in self-sabotage. To understand how a person advances toward death is to approach an understanding of life through its murky mirror image, which has philosophical and practical value for those who love and enjoy life.

"Self-destructive" behavior is defined as any action that a person engages in that causes him to die physically sooner than he would otherwise. This includes both actual and potential volitional actions.

The Death Instinct

The division of human inclinations into two broad groups—those heading toward "Life" and those moving toward "Death"—was proposed by Sigmund Freud. The concept of the death instinct described the inherent tendency of all living things to revert to a state of total inertia. This tendency was fought by two main mechanisms. First, there were instincts present inside the organism that aimed to prolong life and create greater unities of living things. Procreative sexual activity is one example of these.

The second external factor that interfered with the death instinct's functioning was the individual's society, which has its own unique pressures and ideals. The person's killing instinct was prevented from developing into its inevitable manifestation by these factors. Freud believed that at the most fundamental level, these ego forces serve the death instinct, competing to kill the individual. These external forces are now frequently destructive in nature and can withstand the ego forces of an individual.

The General Strain Theory

Robert Agnew created the general strain theory, a criminology concept. The General Strain Theory by Robert Agnew is regarded as a sound theory that has amassed a substantial body of empirical evidence and has also broadened its primary scope by providing explanations for phenomena other than criminal behavior.

Agnew acknowledged that the Robert King Merton strain theory had certain limitations in terms of completely comprehending the variety of potential social stressors, particularly for young people. Merton claims that innovation happens when society promotes socially desirable and accepted goals but simultaneously offers insufficient opportunity to accomplish these goals using legal, institutionalized ways. In other words, those people of society who are experiencing financial hardship but yet desire to succeed financially turn to crime in order to accomplish socially desirable ends. Agnew agrees with this premise, but he also argues that there are more elements that influence criminal behavior in young people. He contends that stressful events other than those brought on by money might also cause stress.

Agnew's three classifications of strains:

The inability to fulfill objectives that are highly regarded

Removing or threatening to remove stimuli that people value highly

To endanger someone by exposing them to unpleasant or poorly regarded stimuli

Agnew and Broidy examined the gender disparities in how people perceive stress and react to it in an effort to understand why male criminality is more common than female delinquency.The degree of tension that each gender endures was the first topic that was investigated. Agnew and Broidy's stress research shows that women frequently endure as much stress as men do. Females also typically experience higher levels of subjective distress. Agnew and Broidy looked into the various strains that men and women face because women endure more strain and commit fewer crimes.

Joiner's Theory (Thomas Joiner, 2005)

The "Interpersonal Theory Of Suicidal Behavior" is another name for it. It contends that a person cannot commit suicide or commit any other form of self-harm unless they have the will and the means to do so. People develop the desire for Death when they maintain two distinct psychological states in their minds at once for a sufficiently enough period of time. Perceived burdensomeness and a sense of poor belongingness, often known as social alienation, are these two psychological conditions. The theory states that fearlessness of pain, injury, and death is something that people who have repeatedly experienced painful and other provocative events, such as previous self-injury and self-destructive/suicidal states, acquire. Self-preservation is a strong instinct that few people can overcome by willpower.

Models of Self- Harm

Chapman, Gratz, and Brown's Experiential Avoidance Model

Any attempt to avoid or flee from one's own experiences or the circumstances that give rise to them is known as experiential avoidance.

Experiences: ideas, emotions, or bodily sensations

Avoidance tactics: substance abuse, DSH, and thinking suppression

Since avoiding causes less immediate discomfort, avoidance is adversely encouraged. After experiences, this relationship grows quite strongly.

Long-term thought suppression usually results in increased distress, an increase in the frequency of troubling thoughts, and an increased chance of a rebound reaction from the emotional experience that was suppressed (i.e., momentary respite results in increased anxiety). Avoidance reduces the possibility that unwelcome emotions will go away and keeps the person from understanding that, while being unpleasant, aversive emotional states are not dangerous.

Freud's Iceberg Model

According to Freud, physical symptoms are frequently the outward signs of deeply repressed tensions. He was implying a radical new explanation of the very nature of the human psyche. In his topographical model of the mind, which he created in 1900 and 1905, Freud detailed the features of the structure and operation of the mind. Freud compared the three levels of the mind to an iceberg when describing them. It is believed that awareness, which is just the top of the iceberg, is made up of the thoughts that are currently the center of our attention. The preconscious is made up of everything that can be remembered. The unconscious is the third and most significant zone. Here are the mechanisms that underlie most behavior and are its true origin. The most significant portion of the mind is the bit you cannot see, akin to an iceberg.

The unconscious mind serves as a storage area, a "cauldron" of instinctive desires and impulses that the preconscious area channels and suppresses. For instance, Freud (1915) discovered that some wants and situations were sometimes too painful or frightful for his patients to accept, and he thought that such information was hidden away in the unconscious mind. Repression is a method that allows for this.

The unconscious mind is significant, as stressed by Sigmund Freud, and the unconscious mind controls behavior to a greater extent than is generally believed.

Emotion Regulation Model of Self – harm

Individual risk variables (emotional reactivity and intensity) and contextual risk factors (invalidating situations that don't provide instruction in emotion regulation skills) work together to create emotional dysregulation.

Self-harm may develop into a coping strategy for intense or uncontrollable emotions. It might be able to help calm anxiety.

Release stress Release rage

Give the impression of control

Put your thoughts to rest.

Put an end to dissociation.

Concretize your feelings of remorse or loneliness and let them go

CHAPTER THREE

Turning Self-Sabotage Into Self-Mastery

You will encounter situations in life that will set you on one of two pathways, either self-destruction or self-mastery, or possibly both. It may not be entirely your conscious efforts that led you to choose one over the other. When a cozy bubble is expanded too far, as is the case with many self-destructive behaviors, people destroy their chances of success since they may not be aware of any better options.

At first glance, self-sabotage might be a result of low self-worth, lack of self-assurance, self-hatred, or a lack of willpower. Actually, the self-destructive behavior is just satisfying the existence of an unconscious urge. You must go through a lengthy psychological excavating process in order to overcome this. To recover from trauma, you must identify the traumatic incident, let go of unprocessed emotions, find healthier ways to meet your needs, change the way you see yourself, and cultivate skills like emotional intelligence and resilience.

Letting yourself have as much time as you need to cry, vent, and let any pent-up energy inside of you that's ready to break out is the first step in moving towards mastery instead than sabotage. The idea is to move forward knowing you don't want to stand in the wreckage of your former life after you've let it go. Realizing that going through this release is the turning point for developing a better self-image and life helps you move forward. Before you can advance and become a master, you must let go and heal. We all experience it at some point on our journeys; it is simply a part of the process. It just depends on how long the healing process takes before you feel ready to let go of the past and build a future filled with success, happiness, and positivity.

If you start to self-sabotage yourself, success is usually just a few steps away. It could be that you're not accustomed to your newfound success because of this.

You decide to sabotage yourself in order to return to where you were previously because it's presenting a picture that doesn't fit with your prior experiences. This is common, and many people choose to give up or do things that hinder their own potential just when they are about to make a breakthrough. The mind is incredibly strong, and if you harbor negative thoughts or have predetermined boundaries regarding what you're capable of or ought to have in your life, as soon as you go beyond those limits, if you're not consciously open to new growth and success, the mind will steer you back toward what it already knows and feels comfortable with. Even though you are capable of handling it, the promotion you deserve may come with additional duties or labor. Even though it would improve your life and better match you with better chances, you choose to make poor choices and pass up the opportunity. Financially, academically, or in terms of relationships. If you can't see it, you won't believe it. You can never succeed if you don't believe it.

Building something new is the best way to advance. By making an effort to think better ideas, utter positive words as much as you can, and take new actions when possibilities present themselves. You'll start to get over the obstacles that seem to be put in your path unconsciously. Your manner of thinking, speaking, and acting will be transformed in order to help you live your best life and reach your full potential. This is not a simple undertaking, but by staying mindful and present, you may maximize what is in front of you and act rationally while making decisions that could either result in sabotage or mastery.

Understanding that you cannot simply deny or ignore your feelings is a sign of emotional intelligence. By repressing them or ignoring them, they won't ever go away. People who behave in this way lack the necessary coping skills to manage their emotions in a responsible manner. To better respond and benefit from each experience that is brought about by those emotions, it is better to confront each feeling objectively and learn from it.

Stoicism is one perspective, but holding your emotions in can sometimes be harmful. It's important to strike a balance between the two. You can then decide when and when emotions should correctly surface. A lot of emotions will make you quite irrational. You will be completely emotionless and robotic. Although you must express your feelings, do not let them rule your actions. Your emotions will be reactions you choose to have instead of impulses brought on by reactions you are letting to happen if you are present and conscious. Never react; always be responsive. You have little influence over how your instincts behave when the mind is not in the present. Your instincts may cause you to feel pleased, sad, or angry. You will decide whether such emotions are appropriate for the moment because you are a more intelligent entity than just an instinctual one. Though it might not be preferable to express them, it doesn't imply that you won't feel them. Everything depends on where and when these feelings appear.

Realize that many individuals never arrive there and hardly acknowledge the fact that they are the ones making the waves in their lives, and it is their responsibility to learn how to ride them as well. Most people struggle to manage or organize their thoughts and feelings, which causes them to become lost.

Understanding your abilities to scale the obstacles in your path is the definition of mastery. Climbing these mountains to uncover your latent qualities, which will be a part of the new you who is destined to be great, is the bittersweet part of life. But if you decide not to persevere, you will regret never discovering how extraordinary you were meant to be.

Understanding your deeper self, which has been telling you for years that you are capable of more, deserving of more, and intended to change into the person you dream of, is mastery.

Everything else will be affected by your healing process. It must be claimed and built. You have to alter internally if you want to change. You must alter how you approach the path if you want to climb the tallest mountains. You'll be able to look back when you've reached the top and realize that each step was worthwhile. Since it wasn't meant to hurt you as much as it was meant to teach you, you will be incredibly grateful for the agony and suffering that motivated you to start your path.

CHAPTER FOUR

11 Ways to Master Your Inner Game

1) Meditation

One of the best methods for achieving calmness and harmony in your mind, body, and soul is meditation. The mind may align the subconscious and conscious minds to manifest whatever your heart wishes with this age-old technique. This method of clearing your mind so that you may reflect objectively on thoughts as they come and go will help you reflect and detach from trauma or prior events that are preventing you from moving forward. Depending on what your intentions are, meditation can be both concentrated and unfocused. Depending on how you approach each practice, it may be incredibly calming or enlightening. It can feel quite peaceful and laid-back at moments, intense and full of tears or laughter at other times. In either case, it's one of the best methods to tap into the inner divine knowledge and intuition you already possess. Reflection, healing, growth, and positive flow are all goals of meditation. Your subconscious will make clear all you need to see and work on. It will be very difficult for you to think clearly and steadily, or to understand the signals the universe is attempting to convey to you, if you are not in the moment. Being open and free-flowing will help you come closer to your divine destiny while you practice meditation.

2) Self-analysis, goal-setting, and journaling

The way to engrave, erase, and keep track of intangible goals is by journaling. Whether it's objectives, positive affirmations, bad habits, or regular stress levels. For you to become a better version of yourself for today and tomorrow, it is essential to write down each of these and think on them. It is essential to reflect in order to develop and learn. How would you know what changes to make if you never thought anything through? Many people disregard this stage and assume that everything will work out on its own. However, in order to make it permanent, you must practice it, just as with anything else. The finest method for ingraining new ideas into the mind, particularly the subconscious mind, is journaling. The challenging aspect is that. It can be difficult to alter the portion of your mind that is made up of all the things you have ever gone through or lived in during your journey. It takes 60 days to break a habit, just as it takes 30 days to form one. Therefore, watch what habits you form because it takes twice as long to break them. Because the brain prefers things that are unchanging, it can carry out these duties with ease. Because you have to actively maintain your new habit, it can be challenging to do so. It feels incredibly dull and tiring since the subconscious mind has not yet been engraved. However, after you've developed a habit, it will require relatively little effort to balance and stay upright on your course, much like riding a bicycle. However, you will need to be really concentrated on the subject at hand when you are first learning, lose concentration, stumble and perhaps get harmed. So just be aware that you will inevitably fall a few times as you establish new habits, but as long as you get back up and keep riding, soon you will be riding hands-free and reaching destinations you never imagined you'd be able to. Reflect, write in a journal, make goals, and simply be consistent. Your strongest allies for success will be repetition and consistency.

3) Face your feelings and express them.

Though emotions are a part of what makes you human, they do not have to rule your life. Throughout your lifetime, you should put a lot of effort into developing your emotional intelligence. If you are not intelligent in this area, you will suppress your feelings and have no control over the emotions you express. It will feel natural to duplicate a feeling for better or worse if you are unable to stop yourself when someone else around you displays it. This explains why being in the company of cheerful people is simple. In addition, feel sad or furious when near disturbed people. The higher the wavelength of an emotion, the more pleasurable it is. Emotions are energy waves with distinct frequencies. The wavelength decreases when an emotion becomes more unpleasant. Therefore, whether you feel joy, love, or happiness, you feel as light as a feather compared when upset, depressed, or spiteful, to being too weighty and hard as a rock. Any repressed energy that has to be let out is released when you talk about your emotions. You will eventually explode if you don't let it out. The people with the strongest mental fortitude allow themselves to be open and vulnerable in order to recover and go on. Talking about your feelings takes guts and fortitude, but once you do, you'll understand that it feels much better to do so than to bury them. If you want to dominate yourself, learn to rationally and under control communicate your feelings. Release any pent-up emotions as well so that you can be upbeat and light as a feather.

4) Modify your language and inner dialogue

The way you talk to yourself greatly influences how you see yourself. Speaking favorably will result in more positive interactions with other individuals. If you speak poorly of someone, you will instead have more unpleasant interactions with them. Whatever is within of you is just reflected in the universe. Love yourself first if you seek love. Be still if you want patience. To find joy, act carefree like a child. Everything you encounter on the outside is a result of your inside views and thoughts. Some people grasp the day when they notice the sun shining brightly. Some people hardly perceive it and feel trapped in the shadows. All of this is based on the individuals' inner language and self-talk. Many people appear to be quite attractive to others, but when they look in the mirror, they are obsessed on some flaw because of what other people think, making them uncomfortable and repulsed by what they see. This could have disastrous results... Additionally, some people who are considered unattractive may feel so comfortable and true to themselves that they walk around carefree and calm. Your exterior language will be determined by your internal language. Expect the universe to respond to your harsh and sharp remarks with harsh and sharp consequences. Expect the universe to return compassion and delight if you speak softly and sweetly. Now, this does not imply that everyone will be pleasant or accept you. They won't be able to equal your frequency, therefore they will have to boost their vibration to match yours or feel the urge to avoid you. When someone tries to be sly or disrespectful, kill them with kindness and make fun of them to observe how unhappy they become. They will make fun of you if you give them what they want, which is for you to become agitated and lower your energy. Take a lesson from this, and always remember to laugh it off. Always go for kindness, but don't take crap! Speak kindly to yourself and exercise mental self-discipline if you want a good life that you can control. Everything in your life stems from the thoughts you have.

5) Let the past go

For a positive outlook and your healthiest way of life, letting go and detaching are essential. A heavy load that weighs you down and limits your growth will result from holding onto anything for an extended period of time. Your history is merely a component of your path, which is intended to instruct and mold you into the person you were meant to be. Failure and trauma increase resiliency and strength, enabling people to approach new problems and pursuits with even greater insight and knowledge. Yesterday is always in the past, and today is a brand-new day. Whatever occurred, take a lesson from it, find healing, develop, and continue. Adjust as necessary and try again. Doing great things imperfectly until you eventually master them is the secret of life. Nobody is flawless, and by criticizing yourself for the faults of others or your own actions, you only make it more difficult for yourself to lead a happy and healthy life. Let go of what you can't control, and focus only on the present moment. Focus on one activity at a time, pay attention to the little things, and be thankful for any chance you are given today if you want to succeed. Don't let your thoughts wander to the past so that you can lose the chances that will bring about the tomorrows you're trying so hard to accomplish. Because you never know when you'll look back and discover you forgot to appreciate the road, be in the now and take it all in. You only have time, and regrets are quite bitter. Utilize today to its fullest and place your brick as skillfully as you can.

Every day, every brick, one by one. Over time, you'll build the ideal path that anyone may follow to learn how to make their own.

6) Develop a fresh perception of yourself

Draw a mental picture of how you want to feel, act, think, and think when you are the new you. Before laying out a plan for how you're going to get there, you need to picture yourself in that position. Even if it's only in the form of a mental image, the mind needs to see it in order to do it. When you start to see small victories and subtle changes in yourself that are beginning to reflect the new you that you're attempting to develop, having a focus on what you're working toward will give you the energy and desire to keep going in that direction. Everything you want to build in life must first begin in your head. While others could have a concept or wish to see you develop, until you see it and make the necessary efforts, it will only be a dream. Dreams come true when thoughts and deeds are in harmony. You need to start working out, listening to gurus, and reading books to increase your knowledge if you want to be stronger, wiser, and smarter. Thoughts are good, but reality is manifested via actions. Because of this, developing the new you takes time and effort, not merely thinking about it once and expecting it to materialize. You must always focus on improving yourself and reminding yourself of the person you want to become. Speak to yourself as though you already possess the qualities, characteristics, or affirmations. In an effort to support you in becoming the new you, your subconscious mind will strive to coordinate with your conscious thoughts. Compared to self-sabotage, which doesn't think it has arrived or will succeed. You must talk to yourself as though you are already who or what you are attempting to become. This is essential for assisting things to materialize with repetition and time.

Let your thinking guide you through difficult and choppy waters while letting your heart paint the best and brightest picture of who you are.

7) Work on your areas of weakness.

You will never reach your entire potential if you simply focus on improving your strengths. The prospects for exponential growth and the development of a better balance among your skills and attributes that support your success or forward movement toward accomplishing anything you seek will be made available by working on your deficiencies. Most individuals enjoy doing what they are good at, but they avoid trying or working on what they are not as good at. Any wonderful thing is worth doing badly at first until you grow better at it. To be truly excellent at something, you need to put in a lot of effort, be consistent, and practice. Your existing talents may have evolved because you were more driven to develop them or because you were merely born with them. In either case, getting to your current level of proficiency and ability required work and time. Some people might be excellent listeners yet struggle to express clearly and with integrity. The only way to improve as a speaker is to put some effort into it. Possibly through participating in trivia contests, literature groups, sports teams, and a lot more. Perhaps enrolling in a public speaking course at the nearby college. Regardless of the method you use to develop your abilities, you must always be willing to try new things and fail. Everybody must experience learning curves in order to reach their potential. Without flaws, everyone would be the same, but we know this isn't the case because each person is different and we can all support one another in growing in various areas of our lives. If you're a powerful speaker but a poor listener, share with a great listener who aspires to be a stronger speaker because sharing is caring. By utilizing one other's abilities, you both become stronger individuals who are better able to take on new challenges and pursue your passions with even more confidence and aptitude for success.

8) Assemble a solid group of allies.

When things get difficult or when you earn a pat on the back, having a team is essential for keeping your spirits up. A strong support network enables you to believe that your success or failure is not just related to you but also to everyone who has invested time and effort in your accomplishment. It will serve as a powerful motivator for you to maintain your drive and ambition in order to realize any objectives or aspirations you may have. When you are concentrated on a team goal, you always perform better. Create a team with people who share your values so that you can all work toward the same objective if you want to be more selfless. By doing this, other people will encourage and inspire you to maintain your resolve and optimism in the face of difficulties. Additionally, you'll be motivated to work harder because you don't want to let the team down. When you are only focusing on your own objectives, it becomes quite simple to take breaks and put things off. Because you alone have those particular objectives. But maintaining a team focus enables everyone to move forward and receive the encouragement or support they require when they do. Recall that your vibe comes from your tribe. Surround yourself with businesspeople if you want to be an entrepreneur. Surround yourself with millionaires if you want to become one. It's that easy. Since people are excellent at reflecting their surroundings, you will unavoidably pick up the patterns and characteristics of the people you spend time with. Make the correct circle of friends or acquaintances that will point you in the direction of whatever you want to become or keep. Everyone will have individual objectives, but having a larger team goal will point you in the right way so you can accomplish your specialty goal inside that team goal.

9) Recall that you are only human.

Nobody is flawless... No one has accomplished great things without facing obstacles, failure, and adversity. Their tenacity, fortitude, and will to advance set those who succeeded apart from those who failed. The most successful people are more eager to try than most people are to fail... That's not good. But they are aware that the payoff is waiting at the other end. Because of this, they're prepared to endure discomfort, endure suffering, and make sacrifices in order to conquer their inner game. Recognize that even if your mind is trained to undermine itself now, you will eventually be able to control it. Simply said, you must be prepared to put it to the test.

Spend the time necessary to develop a calm, collected, aware, and consistent mind since doing so will help you excel in all areas of your life. Because fear is linked to perfectionism, letting up of perfection allows for so much more room for growth, which may arise from the dread of failure, the fear of incompetence, or the fear of prior experiences, will never allow you to take the first step outside of your comfort zone. You must confront your concerns, but you must also let go of the notion that you must or are flawless. You actually perform better and accomplish more when you don't put as much pressure on yourself. Try your best, unwind, and only make necessary revisions. All you can do is that. Be prepared to put in a lot of effort and make errors if you want success. Just don't let carelessness—which is just choosing to be absent and unprepared—be the cause of failure. Failure to plan is planning to fail. Take things one day, one task, and one step at a time. Rome and you weren't both constructed in a day. Your pursuit of perfection is simply limiting you. Break out of this mentality and put up your best effort; from there, everything will come together as it is supposed to.

10) Perfection is a myth; practice makes perfect

The adage "practice makes perfect" is false. Everyone makes mistakes; as I've said previously, even the very finest people in every discipline. The permanence of practice as in the mental processes, daily routines, approaches, skills, and mental attitudes. You will gain knowledge, experience, and wisdom over time, which will help you better grasp how to pursue your passion with grace, certainty, consistency, and success. Common logic dictates that you get better the more you do something. But if you repeatedly perform something poorly, you won't necessarily get better at it because your practice isn't focused on what will lead to success. Superior quality to quantity... You must be present, concentrated, and detail-oriented when practicing a skill. Just be aware that you're putting yourself up for overtraining and possibly regressions if you're eager to accumulate repetition in the belief that it will lead to perfection. A surplus of anything is useless. When your mental capacity is reached, finish what you can today with complete focus and concentration, take a break, and then finish it later today or tomorrow. There is a reason why you need breaks at work; it usually has little to do with your physical health. Over time, your mind needs a break or it won't be as successful at producing quality work. Employers have done their research and are aware of the appropriate times and lengths for employee breaks. If their staff aren't efficient or productive, they'll only be able to offer poor-quality goods or services with less integrity. The mind should only work steadily on one task for 4 hours before taking a break. Anything further won't be regarded as specific or helpful to either party. Even if it takes all day to lay one brick, take your time and make every brick as flawless as you can. Just keep in mind that you will eventually build the best road you could have ever constructed. If you try to rush the process of laying your bricks, you may end up having to start over or experiencing cracks that cause pain and needless work when they could have been avoided by simply taking your time and going with the more sensible course of action. The race is won by the method of slow and steady... Practice makes permanent, whether it's for the better or worse. So be careful what you repeat since it could either lead to exponential success or a fresh start.

11. Thankfulness

Finally, you will retain a healthier frame of mind if you are more thankful. The nicest attitude and highest altitude are produced by gratitude. When aiming for the stars, it's important to be appreciative of all that you have, both possibilities and necessities. You'll have the energy to be joyous and fun in all of your endeavors if you wake up in appreciation. This will encourage you to maintain your optimism when times are difficult and to be ambitious in the pursuit of your objectives. Additionally, if you're on the proper track, it will make the process enjoyable and enjoyable, which should be a part of your trip. Your positive energy will increase as you express more gratitude. Positive energy motivates you to work toward the broader objective and encourages others to lend a hand. Being thankful encourages you to get out of bed and maybe work longer or harder knowing that you have the chance to make the most of the day. Those who truly achieve in life and love their passions possess a gratitude-focused mindset succeeding by pursuing their purpose, living a healthy lifestyle, and remembering that success must be earned, not bestowed. These people are aware that hard work is required for success, and they are also prepared to put in the effort. Being aware of the abundance of opportunities others would kill for... Literally... Because it keeps the mind very present and aids in the removal of unconscious obstructions brought on by missing what is immediately in front of you, gratitude helps eliminate self-sabotage. Every day, remind yourself of the significant and insignificant things for which you are grateful. As a result, you will notice a radical transformation in your outlook, perceptions, behaviors, energies, and reality. Be thankful that you got up today; many people didn't. Remember how fortunate you are to have the opportunity to further your knowledge. Be thankful you can eat today; many people won't. Remind yourself of what you do have in comparison to what you lack, and watch how this will change your perspective and propel you to incredible achievement. The universe will treat you better the more appreciative you are. It all depends on how you think!

Seven Steps to Stop Self-Sabotaging

The "golden larva syndrome" can be caused by a variety of fears, including fear of failure, fear of success, imposter syndrome, perfectionism, and acting like a child. You can, however, take a number of measures to stop this self-destructive behavior.

Acknowledge the presence of dysfunctional behavior

By challenging deeply rooted self-perceptions and resolving underlying issues, take the time to discover what might be hindering you. Try to identify the underlying causes of your self-destructive inclinations; frequently, they can be linked to occasions and experiences from your formative years. Consider the circumstances that make you anxious, and distinguish between real-world facts and emotions that might not be accurate. Every time you experience discomfort as a result of accomplishment, give yourself time to consider the discomfort and assess whether the discomfort is justified.

Reframe your thoughts

Looking at previous "failures" as constructive chances for development and learning might provide a fresh perspective on present and upcoming difficulties. Your reality can be shaped by how you see the world, just as how you talk to yourself can affect how you see yourself.

Self-affirmations that are constructive can change unhelpful thoughts into ones that are empowering and increase your confidence. Recognizing your skills, shortcomings, and the lessons learned from past mistakes will help you change your inner dialogue and adopt a more positive outlook. You should also recognize that setbacks are not life-threatening situations.

Visualize all potential outcomes

Another effective method for preventing detrimental behavior is visualization. Take a moment before acting to consider various outcomes. This will inspire you to visualize the life you want and the actions necessary to turn it into a reality.

Even though worrying about the worst-case situation can be stressful, it can be helpful to realize that the outcome is probably not going to be as bad as you think. Mark Twain, an American humorist and author, expressed it best: "I've had a lot of worries in my life, most of which never happened."

Let go of your inner perfectionist

Set tough but doable goals and recognize that failures and missed deadlines are part of life, not catastrophic occurrences. Try to be fair to yourself and use the power of positive self-talk when you fall short of your own expectations. Change your criteria for success and concentrate on progress rather than perfection.

Stretch your courage muscle

To desensitize yourself to your anxieties, practice saying "yes" to new possibilities, just how exposure treatment is used to treat phobias. To better comprehend your limitations, make a list of the possible ways you are undermining your own success. Recognize that being daring and taking risks is essential for reaching greatness rather than fearing the kinds of opportunities that could perhaps boost your career.

Celebrate your successes

Consider your past victories, acknowledge your role in achieving them, and make a point of rewarding yourself. To keep track of your successes on both a professional and personal level, keep a journal of your accomplishments. Celebrate your successes while forgiving yourself for any faults, and put self-compassion before self-criticism and doubt.

Don't suffer in silence

While self-discovery is essential to understanding what's preventing you from moving forward, there are instances when consulting with dependable people or experts is worthwhile. You can embrace the possibility of achievement and repair the harm caused by self-sabotage with the aid of a coach or psychotherapist.

Additionally, talking to the people in your life about your anxieties will help you learn how others cope with similar difficulties. Talk to them if you discover that some people make you more afraid. Walk away if they won't acknowledge the hurt their actions are doing to you.

Accepting that living entails attempting to be the best version of yourself is the first step toward breaking the cycle of self-sabotage. However, the path to self-actualization also requires that you look beyond your current problems. You can find a sense of fulfillment that extends beyond personal accomplishment by focusing on something greater than yourself, whether it be lending a helping hand to a friend in need, taking part in community activities, or volunteering for a noble cause.

CHAPTER FIVE

Identifying and Overcoming Personal Limitations

Personal Limitations of Different Kinds and How They Influence Us

Personal constraints are frequently characterized as internal obstacles that keep people from reaching their full potential. These restrictions may appear in several forms, such as fear, self-doubt, limiting beliefs, and negative prior experiences. We will examine the many personal constraints in this part and how they may impact us.

Fear is one of the most common psychological obstacles. It might prevent us from attempting novel things, taking risks, or following our goals. There are many different types of fear, including the fears of failure, rejection, and the unknown. For instance, a person who is averse to public speaking may pass up opportunities to speak in front of others, even if doing so could advance their professional or personal development. Fear can sometimes lead to a vicious cycle in which ignoring the fear makes it greater.

Another form of personal restriction that can hinder us is self-doubt. The voice inside of us tells us that we are not talented, intelligent, or good enough to accomplish our ambitions. Self-doubt may result from past events or unfavorable comments made by others. It may also result from a loss of self-worth or confidence. Self-doubt can be sneaky and keep us from taking chances and seizing opportunities.

Deeply rooted thoughts or beliefs that limit us are known as limiting beliefs. They may be conscious or unconscious, and our upbringing, culture, and prior experiences may have an impact. Such limiting ideas as "I am not smart enough to go to college" or "I don't have what it takes to start a business" are just a couple examples. These ideas could become self-fulfilling prophecies that keep us from acting to accomplish our objectives.

Personal limitations can sometimes come from the past. Limiting ideas, anxiety, and self-doubt can be produced by negative previous events, which can keep us from moving forward. For instance, a person who has gone through a terrible event could have anxiety and steer clear of situations that remind them of their trauma.

Personal restrictions can have a significant impact. They may stop us from reaching our objectives, pursuing our aspirations, and leading satisfying lives. Personal restrictions can also lead to negative self-talk, which undermines our self-esteem and confidence. Personal constraints can eventually cause you to feel frustrated, helpless, and despairing.

But it's crucial to understand that these restrictions are temporary. They can be conquered with the appropriate mindset and awareness. Finding the limitation's underlying source and challenging it is one method for doing this. One could start by speaking in front of a small crowd and then progressively increase the size of the audience, for instance, if the limitation is a fear of public speaking.

Reframing negative self-talk into positive self-talk is another tactic. This entails resisting negative ideas and substituting positive affirmations for them.

In conclusion, there are many different ways that personal constraints might manifest themselves, including fear, self-doubt, limiting beliefs, and previous experiences. These restrictions may significantly affect our lives, stopping us from accomplishing our objectives and leading satisfying lives. However, it is possible to get through personal constraints and realize our full potential with awareness and the correct mindset. We can liberate ourselves from the shackles of self-restraint and realize our aspirations by battling against unfavorable beliefs, rephrasing self-talk, and taking baby steps in the right direction.

How to Identify Personal Limitations

Personal limitations can take many different shapes and show up in several aspects of our lives, including our relationships, careers, health, and personal development. These restrictions may prevent us from realizing our full potential, attaining our objectives, and leading satisfying lives. To release our inner force and live our best life, it is crucial to recognize them and overcome them.

Here are some useful methods to help you recognize your own limitations:

Self-reflection: You can use self-reflection as a potent tool to better understand your ideas, feelings, and behaviors. It can assist you in locating behavioral habits that might be restricting your development and impeding your advancement. Find a place that is calm and comfortable, set aside some time, and think on your experiences, thoughts, and deeds to practice self-reflection. What are my advantages and disadvantages? and other related questions. What fears and apprehensions do I have? "What patterns of behavior do I notice in myself?

Request comments from others: At times, we might not be aware of our limitations, therefore doing so can give us a fresh perspective. Get advice about your skills and shortcomings, potential growth areas, and places for improvement from friends, family, coworkers, or mentors. Be receptive to criticism that is constructive and seize the chance to develop.

Examine your previous experiences: Our views, attitudes, and behaviors might be influenced by our past experiences. You can better comprehend how your present constraints were influenced by your past experiences by looking back on them. Consider the challenges you have faced, the moments that have inspired you, and the experiences that have influenced your ideas and values. Examine the takeaways from these encounters and consider how you may use them in the present.

Take personality and aptitude tests: These tests can give you insightful information about your potential, shortcomings, and areas of strength. They can aid in your understanding of your innate tendencies, preferences, and skills. To better understand who you are, take a personality test like the Myers-Briggs or Big Five Personality Tests or an aptitude test like the Strengths Finder or Career Key.

Determine your limiting assumptions: Self-imposed beliefs known as limiting beliefs prevent us from realizing our greatest potential. They could include notions like "I am not smart enough," "I don't deserve success," or "I am not good enough." These ideas may be the result of prior encounters, societal or cultural pressures, or even self-doubt. Determine your limiting assumptions and refute them using the facts. For instance, if you feel that you are not good enough, list the evidence that disproves this notion, such as your prior successes, your skill set, and the favorable comments of others.

The next stage is to get past your personal limitation once you've acknowledged them. Here are some doable tactics to assist you in overcoming your individual limitations:

Create achievable goals: By creating manageable goals, you can assist yourself overcome your constraints. Establish objectives that are meaningful, precise, attainable, time-bound, and consistent with your values and vision. Prioritize your goals by dividing them into smaller tasks and ranking them according to urgency and priority.

Create a growth mentality: A growth mindset is the conviction that we can improve our skills and intelligence with effort and commitment. By accepting challenges, learning from failure, and persevering in the face of adversities, cultivating a growth mindset can help you get over your own constraints. Practice seeing your obstacles as chances for development and emphasizing the process above the result.

Make a move: The first step to overcome your own limitations is to act. It can assist you in gaining experience, overcoming fear and self-doubt, and boosting your confidence.

Common Fears That Hold Us Back and How to Overcome Them

All people experience fear naturally, and it acts as a defense mechanism to help us escape danger. Although fear can be crippling and keep us from achieving our greatest potential. In this section, we'll talk about typical anxieties that restrict us and offer doable solutions.

Fear of failure: One of the most prevalent anxieties that prevents people from following their goals and taking risks is the fear of failing. It is the worry that one may fail and suffer unfavorable effects including disappointment, shame, and embarrassment. This dread might paralyze us and keep us from moving on with our objectives.

Reframing our view of failure is crucial if we want to get past our fear of it. Failure is an opportunity to learn, develop, and get better; it is not a reflection of our value or competence. By accepting failure as a necessary component of learning, we may lessen the fear that comes with it and approach problems from a growth mentality.

Another method for overcoming the fear of failure is to divide our ambitions into more manageable, shorter tasks. With this strategy, we may maintain our attention on growth rather than perfection and create momentum for achieving our final objective. It also aids in our ability to overcome obstacles and grow more resilient.

Worry of Rejection: Another prevalent worry that can prevent us from following our goals and developing deep connections is the fear of rejection. It is the anxiety of being despised, shunned, or left behind by others. Self-doubt, low self-esteem, and social anxiety can result from this dread. Recognizing that rejection is a normal aspect of life is crucial for overcoming the fear of rejection. We understand that not everyone will approve of or agree with us. Although we have no influence over how others view us, we do have control over how we handle criticism. We can lessen the effect of rejection on our self-esteem by strengthening our sense of self-worth and self-acceptance.

Practice vulnerability as a method of overcoming rejection anxiety. Being vulnerable means being willing to show our actual selves and to be receptive to criticism and advice from others. By accepting vulnerability, we can strengthen our relationships with others and increase our capacity for empathy and comprehension.

Aversion to change: A typical concern that can prevent us from seizing new possibilities and taking chances is the fear of change. It is the anxiety brought on by uncertainty and the unknown. This anxiety may cause stagnation, complacency, and the loss of possibilities. It is crucial to adopt a mindset of growth and adaptation if you want to get over your fear of change. We may build the abilities and resilience required to succeed in a continually changing world by accepting that change is inevitable. Change can also be seen as a chance for development and self-discovery. Making the shift into doable steps is another tactic for overcoming the fear of change. We can lessen the feeling of overwhelm and worry associated with the shift by making tiny, incremental movements in that direction. To keep on track, we can also enlist the aid of others and create a network of accountability.

Fear of Success: Although it's a less frequent phobia, the fear of success can nonetheless prevent us from reaching our full potential. It is the fear of the obligations and demands that success entails, as well as the fear of being condemned or evaluated for our achievement. This concern can result in missed chances, imposter syndrome, and self-sabotage. Reframing our view of success is crucial if we want to get over our fear of failure. Success is a result of our diligence and hard work, not something to be scared or ashamed of. We can boost our self-esteem and confidence by accepting success and appreciating our accomplishments.

Techniques for Overcoming Self-doubt and Negative Self-Talk

Many people encounter self-doubt and negative self-talk as regular roadblocks on their path to personal development. They may prevent you from working toward your objectives and reaching your full potential. However, there are methods you can employ to stop doubting yourself and pessimistic self-talk.

Determine your tendencies of self-talk: Knowing your self-talk habits is the first step in overcoming self-doubt and negative self-talk. Pay close attention to the ideas that cross your mind when you are faced with a difficult scenario. Do you typically have a pessimistic or positive outlook on life? Are you having rational or irrational thoughts? You can start to confront and reframe your self-talk routines once you have identified them.

Challenge your self-defeating thoughts: Asking yourself whether your thoughts are sensible or irrational will help you stop talking negatively to yourself. Take a step back and make an effort to do an unbiased analysis of the circumstance if you feel your thoughts beginning to turn negative. Query your own evidence by asking, "What do I have that supports this thought?" and "Is there evidence to refute this belief?" You can begin to loosen your grip on negative self-talk by challenging its veracity.

Once you've confronted your negative self-talk, it's time to reframe it in a more constructive way. Try to change your perspective so that you are thinking more about the positives rather than the drawbacks. For instance, try thinking "I'm capable of overcoming this challenge" instead of "I'm not good enough." You can alter how you view yourself and your capabilities by rephrasing your self-talk.

Self-compassion exercises: Practice self-compassion as a method of overcoming self-doubt and destructive self-talk. As you would a close friend or loved one, be nice and understanding to yourself. Recognize your sentiments when you make a mistake or encounter a setback and remind yourself that mistakes are common. You may strengthen your resilience and recover more quickly from setbacks by engaging in self-compassion practices.

Imagining success: One effective method for overcoming self-doubt and critical self-talk is to visualize success. Spend a few minutes every day seeing yourself achieving your objectives. Visualize yourself conquering challenges, realizing your goals, and taking pride in your achievements. You can increase your confidence and motivation to work toward your goals by picturing achievement.

Positive influences: Another strategy for overcoming self-doubt and negative self-talk is to surround yourself with positive influences. Look for encouraging and supporting friends, family, and mentors. Avoid negative or judgmental people because they will only serve to lower your self-esteem. You may create a network of support by surrounding yourself with motivating people who will keep you motivated and on track.

Finally, take time to recognize and appreciate all of your accomplishments, no matter how tiny. Recognize your successes and give yourself credit for your effort and commitment. Celebrating your victories can boost your self-esteem and serve as a reminder of your progress. Additionally, it might support your motivation and goal-focused persistence.

CHAPTER SIX

The Power of Positive Thinking and Visualization

The Science Behind Positive Thinking and Visualization

We can use positive thinking and visualization as effective tools to accomplish our goals and get through challenges. They have the power to alter our attitudes and perspectives, as well as our behavior and results. The concepts of neuroscience and psychology are at the foundation of the science of positive thinking and visualization.

The brain's capacity for change and adaptation in response to experiences and environmental influences is known as neuroplasticity. It serves as the basis for optimistic thinking and vision. Positive outcomes cause us to develop new neural connections in our brain. These pathways strengthen constructive thoughts and feelings while undermining destructive ones. Positive thinking develops into a habit over time, rewiring our brain to think favorably more frequently.

Visualization is the process of forming an internal representation of a desired result. Its foundation is the idea that the brain is unable to tell the difference between a vividly imagined experience and the genuine thing. The same areas of our brain that would be active during an actual encounter are also activated when we picture a happy outcome. Dopamine and other neurotransmitters are released as a result, bringing about pleasant emotions and reinforcing the behavior.

Positive thinking and imagery have been found in studies to significantly improve both our mental and physical wellbeing. Lower levels of stress and anxiety, better moods, and higher resilience have all been linked to positive thinking. It has been demonstrated that visualization improves performance in a variety of situations, including athletics, public speaking, and academic tests.

Basketball players were split into three groups for a study by the University of California, Los Angeles. One group did nothing, one group practiced making free throws, and one group imagined making free throws. Nearly as much as the group who physically practiced, the group that mentally pictured themselves making free throws shown a considerable improvement in their accuracy.

According to results of another Oxford University study, people with chronic pain who saw their suffering decreasing felt less discomfort overall than those who did not.

Relationships and social interactions can be significantly impacted by positive thinking and visualization. Positive thinking increases our propensity to approach social events with positivity and an open mind. Better connections, stronger communication, and more social support may result from this. To be clear, though, positive thinking and visualization are not a quick fix for all of our issues. They do not take the place of activity or effort. While positive thinking and visualization can provide us the inspiration and mindset we need to succeed, it is still up to us to act and make progress toward our objectives. Maintaining a healthy balance between optimistic thinking and realities is also crucial. Overly optimistic expectations can result in disappointment. It is critical to be aware of potential roadblocks and hurdles and to make plans accordingly.

Techniques For Cultivating A Positive Mindset

A positive mindset is a way of thinking that is centered on hope, optimism, and positivity. It is the capacity to find the positive in every circumstance, despite difficulties and hardship. A crucial component of self-improvement is developing a positive outlook because it can assist you in overcoming challenges and achieving your objectives. We'll look at a number of methods for developing a positive mentality in this section.

Practice being grateful: Practicing thankfulness is one of the best strategies to develop a happy mindset. It has been demonstrated that practicing gratitude, which involves focusing on the things in life for which we are grateful, has a number of advantages. These advantages include improved relationships, more happiness, and better physical health. Simply spend a few minutes every day writing down three things for which you are grateful to practice gratitude. This can range from a satisfying cup of coffee in the morning to a helpful friend or relative.

Positive Self-Talk: Speaking positively to oneself is another method for developing a good outlook. By altering our thoughts, we can alter our attitude because our thoughts have a significant impact on our emotions and behavior. Negative thoughts are replaced with positive ones when one uses positive self-talk. For instance, try thinking "I am capable and will give it my best shot" instead of "I can't do this." We can develop a more positive and upbeat mindset by positively reframing our thoughts.

The practice of mindfulness meditation entails paying attention to the current moment without passing judgment. Numerous advantages, such as lowered stress, higher focus, and enhanced emotional control, have been demonstrated. Visualization: Visualization is a technique that involves seeing yourself attaining your goals and experiencing happy outcomes. By frequently practicing mindfulness meditation, you can create a more positive and calm mindset. You can teach your mind to concentrate on the positive rather than the negative by envisioning achievement and favorable outcomes. You may have a more upbeat and hopeful outlook as a result.

Positive affirmations: Positive affirmations are phrases that you repeat to yourself in order to foster optimistic thinking and a sense of empowerment. They can support the development of a more optimistic mindset and combat negative self-talk.

Embrace Positive People: The companies we keep can have a big impact on how we feel about ourselves. Surrounding yourself with upbeat, encouraging, and supporting people will help you develop a good outlook. Look for connections that foster growth, respect, and encouragement in both parties.

Challenge your Negative Beliefs: Our ability to reach our greatest potential can be hindered by our negative beliefs. It's crucial to confront unfavorable beliefs and swap them out for constructive ones if you want to develop a positive mentality. For instance, if you think you can't accomplish a task, challenge that thought by concentrating on your accomplishments and good traits.

Practice Self-Care: Developing a positive mindset requires self-care. Make time for fun activities such as exercise, hobbies, and outdoor time. To encourage a more upbeat and balanced perspective, tend to your physical, emotional, and spiritual needs.

Visualization Exercises for Goal Achievement

By igniting your imagination and forming a distinct mental picture of your desired outcome, visualization is a potent tool that can assist you in reaching your objectives. By visualizing your objectives, you are communicating with your subconscious mind, which can then assist you in attracting the opportunities and resources you require to achieve your objectives. We'll look at some visualization exercises in this section to help you reach your objectives.

Establish a vision board.

You can construct a visual depiction of your objectives and aspirations using a vision board as a tool. You can use a poster or bulletin board and cut out images and words that symbolize your objectives to make a vision board. You may include images of locations you wish to visit, celebrities you admire, or goals you want to realize. Spend a few minutes each day picturing yourself reaching your goals by putting your vision board somewhere you can see it every day, like your bedroom or office.

Mental Practice

A visualization technique called "mental rehearsal" is visualizing yourself carrying out a task or achieving a goal. You can use mental rehearsal to be ready for a particular occasion, like a performance or a job interview, or to see yourself accomplishing a certain objective. Locate a peaceful area where you can unwind and close your eyes so that you may employ mental rehearsal. Utilize all of your senses to conjure up a clear mental image of yourself carrying out the work or achieving the objective. Imagine yourself excelling and experiencing a sense of empowerment.

Guided Imagery When using guided imagery, you follow a script or audio recording that directs you through a particular visualization exercise. You can use guided imagery to help you accomplish a variety of objectives, like lowering stress, enhancing sleep, or boosting confidence. Online guided imagery recordings are available, or you can make your own with a recording tool or app.

Future-oriented Self-Imaging

When you visualize your future self, you picture yourself as the person you want to be when you grow up. Find a peaceful area where you can unwind and close your eyes before using this technique. Visualize yourself in the future, leading the life you desire and accomplishing your objectives. Create a vivid mental image using all of your senses, and see yourself feeling content, fulfilled, and in control.

Positivity in Oneself

A potent approach for overcoming self-doubt and destructive thought habits is positive self-talk. Select a mantra or affirmation that speaks to you personally to employ as positive self-talk, such as "I am capable and worthy of success." Throughout the day, tell yourself the affirmation numerous times while picturing yourself accomplishing your objectives and feeling assured and in control.

Mental comparison

A visualization technique called mental contrasting involves picturing your perfect future and then the difficulties and setbacks that might occur along the route. Locate a peaceful area where you can unwind and close your eyes so that you can employ mental contrasting. Imagine reaching your goals, then think about potential roadblocks and difficulties. Imagine conquering these challenges and increasing your confidence and drive to accomplish your objectives.

Visualization of Feelings

When you visualize your emotions, you can feel the feelings that come with reaching your goals. Find a peaceful area where you can unwind and close your eyes before using this technique. Use all of your senses to construct a vivid mental image of yourself achieving your goals and feeling the wonderful emotions that come with accomplishment, such as happiness, pride, and satisfaction, and allow yourself to completely experience these feelings.

CHAPTER SEVEN

Personal Goal Setting and Achievement

How to Set Smart Goals

Setting goals is a crucial part of improving oneself. We gain focus, direction, and a sense of purpose from our goals. But not all objectives are created equal. Some are nebulous and impossible to achieve, while others are what we refer to as SMART goals—specific, measurable, achievable, relevant, and time-bound.

SMART goals are defined as being specific, measurable, achievable, topical, and time-bound. Let's take a closer look at each component of a SMART target.

Specific: Goals that are specific are concise and unambiguous. It provides answers to who, what, when, where, and why questions. A definite objective should be clearly stated and understandable. A particular aim would be "I want to lose 10 pounds by the end of the month by exercising four times a week and cutting out processed foods," as opposed to "I want to be healthier."

Measurable: An aim that can be measured and quantified. It enables you to monitor your development and assess whether you are moving closer to your objective. It provides an answer to the question of how I'll know when I've succeeded. A more specific objective may be "I want to get better at public speaking," as opposed to "I want to give five-minute speeches without notes in front of an audience of 20 people by the end of the month."

Achievable: An attainable objective is one that is both reasonable and attainable. It establishes a goal that is difficult but not insurmountable while taking into account your current resources and capabilities. Instead of announcing "I want to run a marathon next week," a more realistic goal would be "I want to run a 3K in three months by running three times a week and increasing my distance bit by bit."

Relevant: A relevant aim is one that is significant and in line with your values, interests, and long-term goals. It responds to the query, "Why is this goal significant to me?" Instead of stating, "I want to learn how to play the guitar," a more pertinent aim would be, "I want to learn how to play the guitar so that I can perform at my friend's wedding in six months."

Time: Goals that are time-bound have deadlines. It gives you a sense of urgency and keeps you inspired and concentrated. A time-bound aim would be something like "I want to write a book someday," as opposed to "I want to write a 50,000-word novel in three months by writing 1,667 words per day."

After discussing the elements of a SMART goal, let's look at how to set one.

Find your aim in the first step. What do you hope to accomplish? Be explicit and precise.

Step 2: Outline your objective. Writing down your objective makes it more concrete and real.

Step 3: Verify that your objective is SMART. To make sure your goal is precise, measurable, achievable, pertinent, and time-bound, use the SMART criteria.

Step 4: Divide your aim into more achievable, smaller steps. What precise steps must you take to accomplish your goal?

Step 5: Create an action plan. What precise actions must you take to accomplish your goal? When will you carry out each action? Who will encourage you on your journey?

Step 6: Set a deadline. When do you hope to accomplish your objective?

Step 7: Track your progress in step seven. Keep track of your development and revise your plan as necessary.

In conclusion, creating SMART goals is an effective strategy to accomplish both your personal and professional goals. You can improve your chances of success and maintain motivation along the road by making sure your goals are explicit, quantifiable, achievable, relevant, and time-bound. Remember to make an action plan, track your progress, and simplify your goals down into doable steps. You can accomplish anything you set your mind to if you are focused and determined.

The Importance of Breaking-Down Big Goals Into Smaller Ones

It is simple to get fired up and ambitious when making objectives, reaching for the heavens with lofty and ambitious aspirations. It's crucial to understand that reaching significant objectives is a difficult process that takes time and persistent work. A technique that can boost our chances of success and keep us motivated, focused, and on track is breaking down big goals into smaller ones.

We can benefit in a number of ways by breaking large goals down into smaller ones. First off, it helps us manage and achieve our goals more effectively. We may see a clear road to success when we divide a large goal into smaller, manageable portions, and we are more inclined to act in the direction of our goals as a result. For instance, if we want to write a book, we may make the process more manageable and less intimidating by breaking it down into smaller goals like writing a particular amount of pages per day or finishing a chapter each week.

Second, splitting up large goals into smaller ones can make it easier for us to monitor our progress and maintain motivation. It can be difficult to observe progress when we have a long-term objective, especially in the beginning. However, if we divide it up into smaller objectives, we can monitor our progress and recognize tiny victories, which can increase our desire and help us persevere. Setting modest goals, such as running for 30 minutes every day or finishing a 10k event, might help us stay motivated and monitor our progress if, for example, our goal is to complete a marathon.

Thirdly, reducing large goals down into smaller ones can enable us to foresee probable difficulties and difficulties early on. We can predict potential obstacles and create solutions when we have a clear plan. For instance, if we want to lose 50 pounds, adopting smaller goals like cutting back on sweets or getting more exercise might help us identify potential barriers like a hectic work schedule or social commitments and come up with solutions.

However, it can be difficult to divide large goals into smaller ones. It can be difficult to know how to divide a large goal into smaller ones, and we might feel discouraged or frustrated if we don't see results right away. But by employing practical goal-setting techniques, like the SMART goal framework, and by remaining motivated and focused, these difficulties can be overcome.

The SMART goal structure, which stands for Specific, Measurable, Achievable, Relevant, and Time-bound, can be used to divide a large goal into smaller ones. Goals that are Relevant are in keeping with our values and priorities, Specific goals are specific and precise, Measurable goals are quantifiable, Achievable goals are attainable, and Time-bound goals have a specific deadline. We may formulate a precise plan and strategy for reaching our goals by using the SMART goal framework.

For instance, if we want to save $10,000 for a down payment on a house, we can divide it into smaller, SMART objectives like saving $1,000 per month for ten months or cutting $500 off of monthly spending to save $5,000 in six months. These more manageable objectives can aid us in monitoring our development and maintaining motivation because they are relevant, specific, measurable, achievable, and time-bound.

In conclusion, it is a strong approach for success to divide large goals into smaller ones. It enables us to detect potential roadblocks and hurdles early on, tracks our progress and keeps us motivated. It also helps us manage and achieve our goals more effectively. We are capable of overcoming obstacles and achieving our goals if we apply sensible goal-setting techniques and maintain our motivation and attention. It's important to keep in mind that reaching larger goals requires time, perseverance, and commitment, but by breaking them down into smaller steps, we can boost our chances of success.

Formulating an Action Plan to Reach Your Objectives

Setting objectives is a crucial first step toward success, but it is only that. You must develop a plan of action that describes the measures you must follow in order to accomplish your goals. This strategy will keep you motivated and focused while giving you a clear path to follow as you advance toward your objectives.

In order to create an action plan, you must first divide your goal into smaller, more doable tasks. This will lessen your sense of overwhelm and make it simpler for you to monitor your progress. Start by listing the precise steps you must take to accomplish your goal. For instance, if your objective is to run a marathon, you might need to increase your weekly mileage, engage in strength training, and maintain a nutritious diet.

After you've determined the steps you need to follow, rank them in order of significance and impact on your ultimate objective. This will enable you to concentrate your time and efforts on the most important actions first. For instance, if you are preparing for a marathon, increasing your weekly mileage would be more important than strength training because it will directly affect your capacity to complete the course.

Setting timelines for each of your action actions is crucial after you've prioritized them. This will ensure that you stay on course and move closer to your objective. Make sure to create reachable, realistic deadlines that will motivate you to strive toward your objective.

It's time to make a plan for carrying out these actions when you've decided on your action steps and deadlines. You may do this by setting aside time for exercise, making a nutrition plan, or finding a training partner who will hold you accountable. Develop a strategy to get through any potential roadblocks or difficulties. For instance, you might need to modify your training schedule to accommodate for bad weather if you're preparing for a marathon in the winter.

As you work toward your goal, it's crucial to keep track of your progress. As you hit each milestone, this will keep you inspired and give you a sense of success. To keep track of your progress and modify your plan as necessary, use a notebook, planner, or app.

Finally, it's critical to maintain flexibility and the readiness to modify your plan as you go. Things might not always go according to plan because life is unpredictable. Always keep your end goal in mind as you remain open to modifying your approach as necessary.

In conclusion, developing an action plan is a crucial step toward realizing your objectives. You may stay on track and advance steadily towards your objective by breaking it down into smaller, more manageable tasks, prioritizing those steps, setting deadlines, developing a strategy, monitoring your progress, and remaining adaptable. You may stay motivated, concentrated, and assured that you are doing the required actions to accomplish your goals if you have a well-crafted action plan.

Tips for Staying Motivated and Tracking Progress

The secret to reaching your objectives and continuing on your path of personal development is to stay motivated. But it's not always simple to stay motivated, especially if you run into roadblocks or failures along the way. Consequently, it's critical to put techniques in place that may keep you engaged and keep tabs on your advancement. Here are some pointers for maintaining motivation and monitoring your development as a person.

Set measurable, defined objectives: Setting precise, quantifiable goals is one of the best methods to maintain motivation. Knowing exactly what you want to accomplish makes it easier to stay motivated and focused. Make sure your objectives are clear and quantifiable so you can monitor your development and gauge your progress.

Divide larger objectives into more achievable tasks: Sometimes we may feel that our goals are too huge or burdensome to accomplish. It's crucial to divide them up into more manageable, smaller jobs because of this. You can see improvement in smaller, more manageable steps, which will keep you motivated and focused.

Honor your accomplishments: Honoring your accomplishments can serve as a strong incentive. Pay attention to and celebrate each accomplishment you make, no matter how tiny. You'll be able to maintain your motivation and optimism as times get difficult with this.

Identify a partner for accountability: Someone holding you responsible for your actions can be a powerful incentive. Find a coach, friend, or family member who can keep you motivated and offer support as you move forward.

Utilize visualization strategies: Utilizing visualization skills can help you stay motivated. Spend some time seeing yourself attaining your objectives and feeling successful. This can keep you inspired and committed to achieving your objectives.

Keep a journal: Journaling is an excellent tool to track your development and take stock of your personal development journey. Goals, successes, obstacles, and any new information you learn should all be recorded. This can keep you inspired and committed to achieving your objectives.

Adopt a good outlook: Adopting a positive outlook will help you stay motivated and laser-focused on your objectives. Look for friends, relatives, or coworkers who can encourage and support you on your personal growth journey.

Use encouraging statements: Encouragement is a great motivator. Spend some time every day telling yourself things like "I am capable of achieving my goals" or "I am worthy of success." This will help you stay inspired and upbeat in the face of challenges.

Seek inspiration from individuals who have accomplished similar goals. This can be a powerful motivation. Attend conferences, listen to podcasts, or read books about personal development. You can learn from those who have gone through similar experiences and maintain your motivation in this way.

Track your development using technology: Monitoring your progress and maintaining your motivation can be facilitated by technology. To keep track of your progress toward your goals, create reminders, or connect with others on a similar personal development journey, use applications or online tools.

You may maintain motivation and monitor your advancement on the road to personal improvement by putting these suggestions into practice. Keep in mind that maintaining motivation is a process, and it's normal to experience ups and downs along the road. Celebrate your victories, take lessons from your setbacks, and keep working toward your objectives.

CHAPTER EIGHT

Time Management and Productivity Hacks

The Importance of Prioritizing Your Time

Time is a valuable and limited resource, and our decisions on how to use it can have a big impact on both our personal and professional life. Many of us lead hectic lives, balancing obligations to our families, friends, job, and our personal interests. Feeling overburdened and as though there are never enough hours in the day to complete everything can be simple. Because of this, setting effective time priorities is crucial.

Making deliberate decisions regarding your time use is the essence of setting priorities. It entails deciding what matters to you the most and directing your time and effort accordingly. By setting priorities for our time, we may concentrate on the tasks that are most important and move closer to our objectives rather than becoming mired down in trivial or irrelevant work.

Identifying your goals and values is one of the most important elements in setting time priorities. What do you hope to accomplish? What is most important to you, both professionally as well as personally? You can acquire clarity and focus on the things that are most important to you by responding to these questions.

After determining your beliefs and goals, you may then organize your time according to those priorities. In order to do this, you must decide how to spend your time based on your personal priorities. For instance, if spending time with your loved ones is a key priority, you can decide to reduce your work hours or assign some chores to others in order to make more time for them.

Realistic expectations about the amount of time you have at your disposal and the duration of particular jobs are also crucial. Many of us have a propensity to overcommit or misjudge how long an activity will take to accomplish. Stress, fatigue, and a sense of perpetual behindness can result from this. You may set more attainable goals and experience a greater sense of control over your schedule by being realistic about the time you have available and the amount of time it takes to finish a task.

Learning to say no is a crucial part of prioritizing your time. Turning down pleas or opportunities can be difficult, especially if they come from individuals we respect or care about. Saying yes to everything, though, might result in overcommitting and losing sight of our values. Learning to say no can be liberating since it frees us up to prioritize our priorities and stop wasting time on activities that don't forward our objectives and core values.

Saying no is important, but so is getting rid of distractions and refraining from multitasking. Distractions abound in our modern environment, from text messages to email alerts to social media updates. As we try to fit as many chores into a day as we can, multitasking can sometimes be enticing. Distractions and multitasking, however, can both result in a lack of concentration and decreased productivity. You may improve your efficiency and do more in less time by removing distractions and concentrating on one activity at a time. Finally, it's critical to prioritize your wellbeing and care for yourself. Many of us put other responsibilities like work or family above our own needs. But ignoring our physical and mental health can result in burnout and a weakened capacity for concentration and productivity. You may enhance your general well-being and your capacity to efficiently manage your time by scheduling time for exercise, relaxation, and other self-care activities.

Techniques For Creating A Daily Schedule That Works For You

It can be difficult to make a daily schedule that works for you. It can be challenging to strike a balance that enables you to be productive without compromising your personal time and wellbeing when you have so many obligations and activities to manage. We'll look at several useful strategies in this section that might assist you in making a daily plan that suits your needs.

Initially, Brain Dump

It can be beneficial to start with a brain dump before you start planning your daily agenda. Write down all the obligations, commitments, and chores that occur to mind over the course of a few minutes. This can include things like work assignments, housework, personal appointments, and anything else you have to do. Prioritizing and organizing your duties is simpler once you have everything in writing.

Set Priorities for Your Work

Prioritizing your tasks is crucial once you have a list of all of them. Decide which tasks are most crucial or urgent, and give them top priority. These should be the items on your to-do list that come first. Think about which jobs may wait until a later time and which ones are time-sensitive and must be finished by a certain day or hour.

Utilize a time block calendar.

A time block schedule is a well-liked scheduling method that entails breaking your day into time blocks and allocating particular tasks to each block. For instance, you might schedule two hours of work-related activities in the morning, an hour of physical activity, and then another two hours of housework. You may better manage your time and stay focused by setting aside set blocks of time for each work.

Consider Breaks

Take breaks frequently during the day to refuel and prevent burnout. Include little pauses in your schedule throughout, such as a 10-minute walk or stretching session in between jobs. This will allow your body and brain to rest and recharge while also assisting you in maintaining focus and productivity.

Be practical

It's crucial to be realistic about what you can do while planning your daily agenda. Avoid packing your schedule with too many things and arbitrary deadlines. If you can't cross everything off your list, this will just cause stress and dissatisfaction. Instead, concentrate on the tasks that are most crucial and order them in that order.

Say no more often.

Learning to say no is one of the hardest aspects of making a daily plan. It's critical to realize when you're taking on too much and master the art of saying "no" to extra responsibilities. By doing so, you'll be able to avoid burnout and concentrate on the activities that matter most.

Be Prepared for the Unexpected

Regardless of how well you organize your day, unexpected things will inevitably happen. It's crucial to leave room in your calendar for unforeseen circumstances or crises. This could entail scheduling additional time in between jobs or having a backup plan in place just in case.

Be willing to make changes

Making a daily schedule is a continuous process, so it's crucial to be flexible. Don't be scared to adjust your schedule if you find that it isn't working for you. To uncover what works best for you, think about modifying your schedule or trying out various approaches.

Review and Consider

Review your schedule each day at the end of the day and think about what went well and what may be improved.

Tips For Overcoming Procrastination and Distractions

The two biggest hurdles that impede people from reaching their goals are procrastination and diversions. They can be a major source of frustration and hinder productivity, which can have an adverse effect on our mental health and general welfare. Success in any area of life, whether it be personal or professional, depends on being able to overcome procrastination and distractions. We will look at some useful advice in this area to assist you avoid distractions and procrastination so you can accomplish your objectives.

Determine the reason for procrastination: Finding the root of your procrastination is the first step in getting rid of it. Procrastination can be brought on by a number of things, including a fear of failure, a lack of enthusiasm, or the absence of specific goals. You can create plans to stop procrastinating by identifying its underlying causes.

Divide tasks into manageable chunks: People often put off doing things because they feel overburdened by the task at hand. Tasks can become less overwhelming and easier to complete by being divided into smaller, more manageable segments.

Set due dates: Setting deadlines can keep you motivated and responsible. You are more likely to prioritize your duties and avoid procrastinating when you have a deadline to meet. Make sure to set attainable, realistic deadlines.

Distractions are one of the main causes of procrastination, therefore eliminate them. Distractions can make it difficult for you to concentrate and complete your work, whether they come from social media, email notifications, or incoming calls. By disabling notifications or using programs that block distracting websites, try to reduce distractions as much as you can.

Utilize the Pomodoro Technique: This time-management technique can assist you in overcoming procrastination and increasing productivity. It entails segmenting your work into 25-minute blocks, with brief breaks in between. You can prevent burnout and maintain attention by using this method. Reward yourself: Giving yourself a reward for a job well done may be a great motivator. Knowing there is a prize at the end can help you maintain your attention and keep moving in the right direction. Make sure the reward is appropriate for the activity you completed and that you will actually appreciate receiving it.

CHAPTER NINE

Building Positive Habits and Breaking Negative Ones

Understanding the Science of Habit Formation

Habits have a significant impact on our life. They are the little, frequently unnoticed things we do every day that add up to a big difference in our success and enjoyment in life. Habits can either support us in accomplishing our objectives or prevent us from realizing our greatest potential. Anyone who wishes to develop good habits and break bad ones needs to understand the science of habit formation. The idea of neuroplasticity is at the heart of habit formation. Neuroplasticity is the term used to describe the brain's ability to adapt and modify itself in response to new experiences. Our brain develops neural connections that make it simpler for us to repeat an action in the future when we repeat it. Because our brain has literally rewired itself to make the activity routine, habits can be extremely difficult to quit.

With a cue or trigger, habit building gets started. This might be a particular moment in time, a particular place, or even an emotion. A habit loop, which has three components (the cue, the behavior, and the reward), is triggered by the cue. The habit itself is the activity, and the satisfying feeling we experience after successfully completing the behavior, is the reward.

Finding the signal that causes the behavior you wish to acquire is necessary for the development of a new habit. For instance, you might leave your gym attire out the night before as a clue if you want to start doing out every morning. Establishing the behavior you wish to foster is the next step. In this instance, it would entail working out every morning for a specific length of time. Establishing a reward for performing the behavior is the final step. This might be a feeling of achievement, more energy, or even a modest reward like a cup of coffee. Once your habit loop has been built, you must keep using it over time. According to research, it takes 66 days on average to establish a new habit. It's crucial to remain dedicated and refrain from interrupting the habit loop throughout this period. When establishing new habits, consistency is essential.

The same habit loop is used to break harmful habits, but in reverse. The behavior, the cue that causes it, and the reward must all be identified. After recognizing these components, you can start to break the habit loop. This can entail altering your surroundings or discovering a new action that offers a comparable benefit. on instance, if you frequently snack when you're bored, you might try taking a quick workout or going on a stroll as a substitute. The emotional and psychological components that can affect habit formation must also be understood. While positive emotions like enjoyment and enthusiasm can facilitate the formation of new habits, negative emotions like stress, anxiety, and sadness can make it more difficult. Our capacity to develop new habits can also be significantly influenced by our ideas and mentality. You're less likely to exert the work necessary to create new habits if you think you can't change.

Techniques for Building Positive Habits and Making Them Stick

Developing positive habits is a crucial component of self-improvement. Habits are strong behavior-shaping forces that can make or break our success. Making habits stick is more difficult than simply creating them, though. The majority of us have been frustrated after beginning a new habit only to give it up after a few days or weeks. In this part, we'll look at several strategies for forming virtuous routines that stick.

Start Little

Starting too big is one of the biggest errors people make when attempting to form a new habit. They simultaneously attempt to change their conduct dramatically and set themselves high standards. Unfortunately, this method rarely works. Start small instead. Select one minor habit you wish to create and concentrate on it. For instance, start off with just 10 minutes a day if you want to begin exercising regularly. Once you've got that down, start lengthening the time.

Be Particular

Make your habit quantifiable and specific. Instead of stating a general objective such as "I want to exercise more," make it more specific by saying something like "I want to walk for 30 minutes every day." Being detailed makes it simpler to track development and maintain motivation.

Connect a trigger to your habit

Connecting a new habit to an existing trigger is one efficient way to do so. Connect a new habit to an existing one, like brushing your teeth, if you want to start flossing every day. After brushing your teeth, floss every time. Over time, flossing will become easier to recall because the act of brushing your teeth will become a trigger.

Use Reward-Based Training

Powerful motivation comes from positive reinforcement. Reward yourself whenever you fulfill your habit effectively. It may be as straightforward as a pat on the back or a tasty treat. Celebrating your accomplishments will keep you inspired and strengthen the habit.

Make a habit tracking tool.

A habit tracker is a tool that you can use to visually monitor your progress. It might be an app, a chart, or a calendar. Mark the habit tracker each time you accomplish it successfully. Keeping motivated and reinforcing the habit will be easier if you can see your progress.

Find a Partner Who Can Be Accountable

Someone holding you responsible for your actions can be a strong incentive. Find a partner in your endeavor and communicate with them frequently. Discuss obstacles, share your success, and encourage one another to form virtuous habits.

Develop mindfulness

The practice of mindfulness involves being totally focused on what you are doing and being present in the present. It can assist you in maintaining attention and overcoming distractions that might prevent you from forming new habits. You will find it simpler to maintain your habits if you set aside some time each day to practice mindfulness.

Prepare for Challenges

Obstacles are a common component in habit formation. Prepare for probable problems by anticipating them. If you intend to work out every day, for instance, make a plan for what you will do if it starts to rain. Making a plan will help you overcome challenges and maintain your habit.

Accept Failure

It's not always simple to create new habits, and failures are inevitable. Be not deterred by failure. Instead, make the most of the chance to improve and learn. Analyze what went wrong and alter your approach. Remember that success is more about overcoming failure than it is about never experiencing it.

Consider progress rather than perfection.

Finally, keep in mind that creating healthy behaviors is a journey rather than a finish line. Consider progress rather than perfection. Celebrate modest victories and take lessons from failures. Positive habits will gradually become ingrained in your everyday routine if you are persistent and patient.

Breaking Negative Habits and Replacing Them With Positive Ones

Habits are actions we take automatically and without realizing them. They can greatly affect our lives and are frequently developed via repeated activities. Our relationships, physical health, and general well-being can all be negatively impacted by negative behaviors. Positive habit replacement can be difficult, but it's a crucial component of personal development.

Identifying a bad habit is the first step in kicking it. Overeating, smoking, procrastination, and negative selftalk are just a few examples of undesirable habits. It's critical to comprehend your unfavorable habit's motivations once you've identified it. Does it serve as a coping technique for anxiety or stress, or is it a result of boredom or a lack of direction? You can address the underlying problem and develop a plan for change by understanding the motivation behind the behavior. Having the discipline and dedication to break a bad habit is necessary. It's crucial to make change plans and set realistic targets. To replace the bad habit with a good one is one useful tactic. For instance, you could substitute a healthy activity, like eating fruit or vegetables, for your bad habit of nibbling on harmful foods. In this manner, you are still able to satisfy your craving for a snack but in a healthier and more advantageous manner.

Another successful tactic is to foster a positive atmosphere. This can involve avoiding situations or triggers that could cause you to engage in the bad habit and surrounding yourself with supportive people. It may also entail asking friends, relatives, or a professional for assistance if necessary. Changing a habit can be difficult, but it can be facilitated by having a support network.

It's crucial to be persistent and patient in addition to replacing bad behaviors with good ones. It takes time to break a habit, and failures are frequent. It's critical to recognize, take lessons from, and move past these setbacks. Celebrating little successes and advancements can also keep motivation and momentum strong.

Positive habit formation is crucial to human development. Positive behaviors can enhance our entire well-being, relationships, and health. Choosing the behaviors you wish to foster is the first step in developing good habits. This could involve anything from consistent exercise to cultivating gratitude to picking up a new skill.

Once you've determined your ideal habit, it's crucial to create an implementation strategy. Making the habit a regular part of your life can be achieved by setting clear, attainable goals and developing a daily routine. Another method for developing a sustaining habit is to start out easy and progressively increase the challenge or frequency of the behavior.

Developing healthy behaviors involves perseverance and self-control. Even when it seems like the habit isn't having much of an influence, it's crucial to continue with it. To keep motivation and momentum going, it can be beneficial to monitor your progress and recognize minor accomplishments. It's crucial to foster a growth mentality in addition to developing good habits. This entails interpreting obstacles and failures as chances for development and education. Adopting a growth mindset can assist you in overcoming challenges and keeping a positive attitude on your own personal development.

In conclusion, developing beneficial habits and breaking bad ones are crucial components of personal development. It necessitates dedication, endurance, and a readiness to adapt. You can break bad habits and replace them with good ones by recognizing them, comprehending the causes, and coming up with a change strategy. Identifying desired behaviors, developing an implementation strategy, and upholding consistency and discipline are all necessary to develop beneficial habits.

You can develop positive habits and experience personal improvement by adopting a growth mindset and surrounding oneself with uplifting influences.

How To Maintain Your Positive Habits Over The Long Term

An effective strategy for enhancing your life, achieving your objectives, and unleashing your inner strength is to form positive habits. However, creating a habit is only the first step; long-term maintenance is just as crucial. In this section, we'll look at how to keep up your good habits throughout time so you can keep enjoying the results of your labor.

Set reasonable goals.

People struggle to keep up their good behaviors for a variety of reasons, including having inflated expectations. If you set the bar too high and don't get results immediately away, you could lose motivation. It's crucial to keep in mind that creating a habit is a lengthy process, and it could take some time before you start to reap the rewards. Set reasonable goals for yourself, and don't give up if you don't achieve results right away.

Salute Your Success Along the road, it's crucial to recognize your accomplishments. Spend some time reflecting on the advantages brought about by your new routines. Celebrating your accomplishments helps keep you inspired and motivated to keep going on your journey.

Put the benefits first

Keep in mind the reasons behind your initial decision to develop positive behaviors. Consider the advantages that your new behaviors are bringing you. This might support your commitment to upholding your behaviors for the long run and help you stay motivated.

Establish a Support System

Long-term maintenance of your positive behaviors can be greatly improved by having a support system. Be in the company of people who will support and encourage you on your trip. Join a group of people who share your goals and are working to better their lives. Having a support system can help you be motivated and accountable.

Monitor Your Development

You can remain committed and motivated to upholding your healthy habits throughout time by keeping track of your progress. To track your development and recognize your accomplishments along the way, use a habit tracker.

Establish a Routine

You can keep up your good habits over time by developing a routine. Your habits get embedded in your everyday life when you build a routine, which makes it easier to uphold them over time. Establish precise times for your routines and try to keep to them.

Make necessary adjustments

Remember that there is no one method that works for everyone when forming a habit. Because everyone is unique, what functions for one person may not function for another. Be ready to change your strategy if you discover that it isn't working. Try out various approaches until you discover the one that works best for you.

CHAPTER TEN

Developing Emotional Intelligence and Resilience

Understanding Emotional Intelligence and Why It's Important

The capacity to comprehend one's own emotions as well as those of others and to use that understanding to influence behavior and interactions is known as emotional intelligence. Emotional intelligence is gaining importance in today's fast-paced society as it enables people to successfully negotiate challenging social circumstances, forge better relationships, and succeed in both personal and professional contexts.

Personal competence and social competence are the two fundamental components of emotional intelligence.

Personal competence is the capacity to be aware of and control one's own emotions, whereas social competence is the capacity to be aware of and control others' emotions. Let's examine each of these talents in more detail and discuss their significance.

Personal aptitude

Personal competency includes motivation, self-awareness, and self-regulation. Knowing one's own emotions and how they affect behavior and decision-making is known as self-awareness. It entails being truthful with oneself and accepting one's positive and negative traits. The capacity for self-regulation is the capacity to restrain one's feelings and impulses and to adjust to shifting conditions. It entails preserving a good outlook, remaining goal-focused, and refraining from negative actions like procrastination or impulsivity. Motivation is the capacity to focus feelings in a constructive manner and use them to propel success and achievement. It entails establishing objectives, exercising initiative, and persevering in the face of challenges.

Social Awareness

Social competency includes relationship management, social skills, and empathy. Empathy is the ability to understand and relate to the emotions of others. Active listening, awareness of nonverbal signs, and displaying empathy and understanding are all part of it. The capacity to influence others, establish relationships, and communicate effectively are all social abilities. It entails having the ability to assess a situation and modify one's communication approach as necessary. The capacity to establish and preserve wholesome relationships with others is known as relationship management. It entails having the ability to settle disputes, collaborate, and handle challenging conversations.

The Importance of Emotional Intelligence

There are several reasons why emotional intelligence is significant. It mostly aids people in developing closer ties with others. We are more able to successfully communicate, establish trust, and promote cooperation when we are able to comprehend and relate to the emotions of others. This is particularly significant in the workplace, where successful collaboration and teamwork are paramount.

Additionally, emotional intelligence aids with stress management and coping with challenging circumstances. We are better prepared to handle obstacles and setbacks when we are able to identify and control our own emotions. This is especially crucial in situations of great pressure, where the capacity to maintain composure and focus can make the difference between success and failure.

Last but not least, emotional intelligence is crucial for personal development. We are better able to assess our strengths and limitations and take action to better ourselves when we are able to understand and control our own emotions. This promotes improved self-awareness, boosted self-esteem, and a sense of meaning and purpose in life.

Finally, in today's fast-paced world, emotional intelligence is a fundamental talent that is becoming more and more crucial. We may improve our interpersonal and social skills, manage stress and challenging situations, and succeed both personally and professionally. Although the journey lasts a lifetime, it is well worth the effort.

Techniques for Improving Self-awareness and Self-Regulation

Emotional intelligence is largely comprised of self-awareness and self-regulation. We can clearly grasp our ideas, feelings, and behaviors when we are self-aware. We can recognize our strengths and limitations thanks to this insight, which also enables us to make decisions that are in line with our values and objectives. In contrast, self-regulation is the capacity to control one's emotions and actions in a healthy and productive manner.

Self-awareness and self-regulation can both be improved through a variety of ways. Here are a few of them to consider:

Meditation on mindfulness: Paying attention to the moment without passing judgment is a component of mindfulness meditation. By enabling us to become more attuned to our thoughts, emotions, and bodily sensations, this practice can aid in enhancing self-awareness. We can start to spot patterns and triggers that affect our behavior as we become more conscious of these elements of ourselves. We can better control our emotions and actions by doing this.

Journaling: Writing in a journal might help you become more self-aware. We can find patterns and triggers that affect our behavior by outlining our thoughts and feelings. We may become more aware of our ideals and objectives as a result. We can develop greater self-awareness and improve our ability to make choices that are consistent with our beliefs and objectives by periodically reflecting on our experiences and feelings.

Feedback: Getting other people's opinions can be a great method to increase self-awareness. We can learn more about how others perceive us and the effects of our actions by getting their point of view. This input might show us where we have blind spots and where we can improve.

Mindful breathing is a strategy that entails concentrating on our breath and being aware of our body's sensations. Through stress reduction and nervous system relaxation, this technique can assist us in controlling our emotions. We can improve our ability to manage our emotions by including mindful breathing into our everyday practice.

Self-reflection is a process that entails considering our attitudes, sentiments, and actions. This routine might provide us new perspectives on our motives and ideals. We can develop more self-awareness and make better judgments that are consistent with our beliefs and objectives by periodically reflecting on our experiences.

Practice your gratitude: Gratitude is a strong feeling that can aid in bettering self-control. We can develop a more optimistic outlook and better control our emotions by concentrating on the positive parts of our lives. We can improve our emotional control and self-awareness by including a regular appreciation practice into our daily routine.

Exercise: Exercise is a further effective method for enhancing self-regulation. Endorphins are released during exercise, and they can help us manage our emotions and reduce stress. We can improve our emotional control and self-awareness by including regular exercise in our regimen.

Making better judgments, fostering healthier relationships, and achieving our goals are all made possible by employing these approaches to increase our self-awareness and self-regulation. The development of self-awareness and self-regulation must be seen as a continuous process that calls for practice and dedication throughout time. But by implementing these methods into our daily lives, we can improve our ability to control our emotions and develop a deeper sense of self-awareness.

How to overcome setbacks and cultivate resilience

Our amount of resilience is based on how we handle the difficulties and setbacks we encounter in life. Being resilient is having the capacity to overcome hardship and keep a good view despite it. It is a necessary talent to cultivate for everyone trying to attain their goals and a crucial element of personal growth. Here are some doable tactics for strengthening your resilience and recovering from setbacks:

Exercise self-care.

In order to develop resilience, self-care is vital for sustaining sound physical and mental health. You may keep a good outlook and handle stress better by taking care of yourself through regular exercise, a nutritious diet, and enough sleep.

Create a reliable support system

When it comes to developing resilience, having a solid support system can make all the difference. Call on the friends and family you can trust for moral support and inspiration when things are tough.

Become growth-oriented

A growth mindset is the conviction that your skills and intelligence may be advanced through effort, commitment, and tenacity. You can perceive setbacks as opportunities for learning and growth rather than failures by adopting a growth mindset.

Practice being mindful.

Building resilience and controlling stress can be accomplished with the help of mindfulness. You can learn to better control your thoughts and emotions and achieve a deeper sense of inner peace and tranquility by engaging in mindfulness practices like deep breathing, meditation, and yoga.

Set sensible objectives.

You may prevent feeling overwhelmed and demotivated in the face of setbacks by setting reasonable goals. Larger goals should be broken down into smaller, more achievable steps, and minor victories should be celebrated along the way.

Understanding failure

Life will inevitably involve failure, and developing resilience requires that we learn from our mistakes. Instead of concentrating on your errors, use the time to consider what went wrong and what you might do differently in the future.

Develop a positive outlook

Building resilience requires keeping an optimistic outlook. Focus on the good things in your life, and make an effort to see the challenges as possibilities for development.

Consult a specialist if necessary.

Do not hesitate to seek professional assistance if you are experiencing stress, anxiety, or other mental health issues. You can develop resilience and overcome setbacks with the help of a trained therapist who can provide you the tools and encouragement you need.

Printed in Great Britain
by Amazon

34458131R00076